As Luck Would Have It

MARK WEISS

As Luck Would Have It

Shearsman Books

First published in the United Kingdom in 2015 by
Shearsman Books
50 Westons Hill Drive, Emersons Green
BRISTOL
BS16 7DF

Shearsman Books Ltd Registered Office
30–31 St. James Place, Mangotsfield, Bristol BS16 9JB
(this address not for correspondence)

www.shearsman.com

ISBN 978-1-84861-413-0

Acknowledgements
Some of these poems have appeared in earlier versions in *Poetry Review* (UK), *Poetry Salzburg Review*, *Ecopoetics*, *Tinfish*, and the online journal *Jacket*, as well as other sites on the web. An earlier version of "Different Birds" was published as an ebook by Shearsman Books. "Dark Season" was published as a chapbook by Least Weasel, an imprint of Prosopolis Press.

CONTENTS

III Riffs

IV Different Birds

V Dark Season

for Pearl

I
California Girls

Husbandry

Attention sways, can't fix
to anything.

Every morning he goes to his garden
barefoot, for the cold pleasure. Each day the beans
are taller; the wind
has flattened them against the wire
long enough for a tendril
to take hold
that the vine may climb
toward sunlight. All of it
as if by accident—as if untended: this row of lettuce,
this of beets,
a vagrant clump of weeds, a pile of cuttings. After all,
it's the ratty ends of things
he finds attractive. Little room
to cultivate a life
or a wife.

To accept one's lot may be
to become a pillar of sorrow,
he thinks, but to be alone
is salt itself.

Harvest

In my last New England autumn I played the odds
the night first frost was called for and left
the rest of the tomatoes
unharvested. They survived
somehow, bright summery red
against the firs and grass
in the waning light of my garden clearing,
swamp-maples in the streambed
maples beside it
and the vivid undergrowth in the pine-duff
flaming their various golds and purples.
When I finally plucked them
at the last moment before hard frost, they made a sauce
to last the winter. Now,
in this season of death, my first such,
my father dead, and Bill, and Richard,
I make the yearly sauce across the continent, where nothing
as dangerous as autumn
seems to happen. I think to make
an emblem of that last
harvest before winter,
as if my father and Richard
had not strangled on their own fluids
and lovely, curious and fastidious Bill,
whose presence itself could heal the wounds of childhood,
had not turned hideous in the act of dying.

Feral Garden

Stepped on a dead bird had been stepped on unnoticed
many times, but this time
in socks,
whatever clear fluid wicked up, through
to my skin, cold and greasy. Not much—
a nestling. Pink, naked, beak and feet,
blue eyelid.
Scraped it up from in front of the door
with a piece of paper, its mark
still on the deck,
and into the garbage. But noticed
a pale red stain that had been hidden
beneath its body that must have been
its whole life's-blood.

Hours later
I dreamed I had poked out my left eye
on the sharp edge of the shower curtain
and on the floor
a bloodied globe with a blue pupil for all the world
intact, but useless. And spent my sleep
testing my vision   back and forth
blinking each eye   coming to terms
with my new affliction.

Fell from the nest
found by the possum or the neighbor's cat
and left here? From the other side of
the garden, where my wife has hung
a feeder full of seeds from a bough,
making that space the main hangout
for the neighborhood flyers, doves to sparrows,
and a better prowl
along the fence behind it
for whatever felines. Who

are we feeding
in this wild garden, the small birds
eating their seeds at the feeder
and diving to the tilled ground for insects.
Between us the scattered petunias and peppers.

So let me tell you about my garden.

As Luck Would Have It

Strange, Carlos says, to see the country
beyond the city, a line of hills
in the distance. I'm here,
I could be there, I told myself once
at the open window, two realms
of the possible.

Earlier today at gray noon
a parade of Sikhs followed the van
in which their living saint was carried
through the streets of Glasgow. They wore orange
turbans or shawls and walked
barefoot, the difference between here and Lahore
soon apparent, a choice made
and remade daily.

Sickening at the thought.
Nausea, dread.
Not so much moving towards
as averse to,
as good a way to choose
as any.

That a great wound's behind it may be useful to think
whether true or not.

Maybe there was a voyage to a place that the mind seeks
forever after, that's become—what—heart's-desire, but changed,
so that the voyage can be made now only in dreams, as if
abducted nightly by the wee folk
one had once been one of. I just
didn't want to do it, I did this
instead. What
after the mountains? now just beyond suburbs, the refuge
in hot weather, that banal, where mishap

had enchanted each place water collected, the slow spring
in the field beneath a lone bush
that was never cut, the shed
where the blacksmith worked
chained to his forge,
the bear in its cage,
the mythic sundaes and the catfish
big as your arm, how in a flash
it could all be turned around, a horse
poisoned by clover, a line of houses
become uncanny, somewhere in there
a sort of decision, "I would rather not" or
"I would rather," creating a field
from which the figure
would emerge. What emerges.
But how did I get here,
and how did this field happen?

Translated

In exile do you hear
horrible stories from the homeland and
wring your hands? do you
turn your back and begin to make as they say
a new life?

.

As if body-language had accents,
which it does, the stranger easy to spot
across the field.

But here, watching the Irish barmaid wait for the drink, her arm
folded so that forearm rests against sternum, wrist
curled, her fingers
toying with a necklace.
One would have thought it painful, but the stance
has years of practice behind it,
the line from gesture to dance,
depiction to enunciation.

She spoke the gestures
of her native land.

And that other one did so after three generations.

.

I suddenly find myself imagining
my friends torn, dis-
membered, nightmares
from the evening news,

and imagine last words,
Carlos taking them down
because I'm beyond writing. "I have always been

a harlequin," I say,
too distracted to find the right phrase.

What kind of legacy would that be,
lucky as I've been,
all the sounds of the world to choose from.

.

Always puzzled by the separation of passion from the everyday.
Impossible to imagine the way instinct could erupt
through such lives, clothing itself
a form of refusal.

.

Even now your lips remember
when they were blossoms.
And I remember when I would say
"Your lips are blossoms."

.

Civilization and its discontents.
It's a matter of degree isn't it.
Complicity's the point isn't it.

.

Two kids on a dark porch
court and smoke and cough
across the street, expecting the night
and its breezes to disperse
whatever evidence.

.

Places named for the words first heard there. So
what I call "pomegranate" you call
"ruddy," or "went," and courtship
becomes the exchange of names.
Smitten, how charming that what you call

"haberdasher" I call
"clout," though we both
swim there. Translating desire,
I reach for "cudgel," that mound
you love me to touch, the left one, and its mate,
"compassion."

.

Every word a sort of conquest.

California Girls

This time that gracelessness one would mistake for candor
is merely gracelessness,
and wouldn't it be lovely
to dance
through a lifetime. Gravity
is such a cruel instructor.
What can I say? In the failed
garden I've made this summer
a few blossoms nod on the peas
for all the world like orchids.
One takes one's consolations
where one finds them. Time to admire
the tenacity of weeds.

Renga

Summer? In Sumer
I'd expect it.
But here?

Waver of light rising
off the tarmac.

In such a state
anything,
tire tracks.

…and if I were a bird
I would fly away…

That time
upon us. Big moon
through smoke.

The light, filtered,
stains your face.

Made love
to on
purple duff.

Come out come out come all ye
wherever you are.

Easy to leave
Cheyenne
this morning.

A mountain somewhere
with something on it.

Having pissed, polar bear
is whiter
than snow.

Frozen, Moon River flows
through frozen fields.

Each day the bird
has learned
a different tune.

Repetition
the wild card.

Who wrote who
wrote the
book of love?

Ask her: who wrote, wrought, what? "Which
needs?" she says.

First there is
a mountain
with a white bear.

Fly away, build a nest and shriek
your heart out.

Only bees
can understand
the flowers.

One can refuse to be
reborn, maybe.

II

Glass Palace

—17 Poems

Advice

What you need, he said,
is another trip to the edge
and beyond.

And I thought he was joking.

Ease of Motion

This fantasy that has deluded many,
that you could open the door and walk
into another place,
just like that.

Among the Bulrushes

It must have happened all the time, a woman
giving a child to the river. But the misery, to think
that chance could better care for it—the conditions of famine,
slavery and such—and the fantasy, that the child, rescued,
would come to recognize itself
at the last moment, and free the tribe
from its wretchedness. It must have been that commonplace
to become their story.

A Message to the Gods in the Blood of Sacrifice

"See, we have horses.
Life is good."

A Simile

That red red rose is like my love:
thorns below and thorns above.

Adam and Eve

It's the snake, they think,
that renders tolerable
this insipid garden.

Siren

Moving her legs slowly against the water,
folding it.
In gelid light
small tufts
on either side.

Survival

Shock of the ocotillo's red spear
against the creosote's green and the yellow flowers
of brittlebush. Birds
melodically proclaim
there's a stranger here, while insects,
wild with delight,
bid me welcome as a source of liquid.

And the bees
suck at the mud where the stream
had overflowed its banks.

The King

Oedipus the Riddle Solver becomes the answer
to the plague's question:
"What sleeps with his mother
and murders his father?"

Exile

The pace of change being what it is
the homeland you dreamed of
is no longer there.
Like Troy to the Trojans, no stone
left as a marker.

Focus

Whose greatest worry was to paint the petal
just so.

A decent restraint,
when the moon seems the largest thing.

His Will

Stunned into numbness,
numbed
into silence.

Who could have imagined
any of it?

A Simile

Tastes like rabbit, the fox thinks,
slinking from the hen-house.

Horse Sense

There's many a slip
twixt the clop and the clip.

We call it luck
to die by increments.

A Story

Dressed for the bridal bed
her shawl became the sky, her gown
the sea.

Glass Palace

I imagined a broken glass thing
inside me.

My grandmother had a clock
built of mirrors in the form
of a palace. In my first
memory it was broken
and dangerous.
Lovely, the way it glinted.

This was the broken thing
I had imagined.

And So

You may go on to other things
now that you understand the mysteries.

The daily miracle and the daily curse.

Something about the dance
or stagger
of anxiety.

III

Riffs

Wheelbarrow, For Williams: I

1

In my dream I was wheeling a red
wheelbarrow. There were chickens
everywhere, white
as stars—silent,
and soft,
and pleasant to look at.

2

The hen must be white
to cleanse properly. And it was,
a gentle creature, surprised at its fate
and questioning
in the language of chickens.
After he had removed whatever curse
from us Armando
slit its neck and fed the blood
to the goddess.

3

When my shoulder mends
I will go to the farm
where they raise chickens in a long
warehouse and fill a wheelbarrow
with their droppings
for my garden.
And think of the bird
in far-off Cuba, dead,
for whatever ailed me.

Wheelbarrow, For Williams: II

1

Two barrows had I, red,
and green. The chickens roosted
in the red, so I bought
the other. And they roosted there
as well. Now my yard is filled
with barrows.
Under each
white hen
a clutch of eggs,
some white
some brown.

2

To a chicken a wheelbarrow
must be like the back seat
of my father's chevy.
Add straw, and
what a ride!

3

Hey Flossie! See
what the chickens
are doing!

Wheelbarrow, For Williams: III

1

Someone has painted the wheelbarrow
with raspberry jam. The chickens
have discovered the seeds,
and peck furiously, a frantic din,
like music. Not good
for bird or barrow—the first
blunted, the second
dented. And the hens
flecked with red,
part preserve,
part blood. They were white
they were white
but now are sullied.
No eggs tomorrow.

Perhaps it was the god who did the painting.
Now there will be death
and insects
and a world of changes.
Who would have thought
so much
could depend upon
a red wheelbarrow?

2

There was a gaiety
to those shiny red things.

The Passing Sound

The remnant of a structure once projected.
As common
as a swarm of bees.

No room for accident
except the slip of the brush.

Slight articulation of a joint.

Did she really
say that?
what?
as if every tee uncrossed became an ell.

Reducing a dance to a set of poses.

Reporting all the symptoms.
A woman's voice behind the curtain:
"It was in the groin,"
she says.

There Appears to Be an Iconography

1
Top dog
gets the window.

.

I imagine myself dead
and cry out: "shape?
shape?
What are you talking about?"

.

A balm for all sorrows,
a shelter from rain.

.

The fantasy
that there are others
despite the evidence.

.

"I've never seen you eat like this,"
she says, excited
that there's something
she's never seen.

2
Clean, sturdy feet, and all her toes
point in the same direction.

.

Here with a glance
is the message I bring you:

that even men your father's age
will want you.

.

In a wheelchair now. "What I noticed,"
he says,
"is the way she walked."

.

The deaths of thousands less
than one death multiplied.

3
Democratic violence—
each with his own
thunderbolt.

.

This little tough guy's tyranny directs
his mother, Go! Stop!
as if commanding a dog.
He knows his way around.
Moment to moment
he saves her life.

.

On the crowded bus I stumble backwards.
Apologizing, I turn
to the tall man who over and over
touches his fingers together.

4
In a previous dream I had seen this masterpiece. Flaglike,
thin stripes
of orange, green,

yellow, red, so beautiful
there was nothing to say.

When I awoke after the auction I was filled
with sorrow–had I forgotten
to bid and lost it–before it came
to me that I had seen it only
in an earlier dream.

Flaglike, its impossibly light colors
soiled, creases here and there, the paper soft,
the margins tattered.

.

The bloodiness of Medusa's haircut, the barber
following the sway of hairs and pouncing
at the last moment,
the floor covered
with darting tongues.

Aie! Aie!

.

"Happy the man
who lives in boring times."

Someone
should try it.

.

"*Frac   Frac*"
Over and over the brain
spits it out
the r rolled
like a machine gun
frac frac
how it ends
frac

frac frac the machine
barking.

.

I dreamt of death.
Soon enough.
Why bother?
Like a snake tasting the wind.

Riffs

Affirmation.
Made solid.
Contract.
A signature.
Signed off on   off/
on.

Reaffirmed
all over again.

*

John Hancock.   Hand
cock? half
cocked?
Crockery?
Language
as real as grass
or glass.

*

Career.
A wild ride.
So it turns out we find ourselves half way through
the one career.

*

Oration.
A golden prayer or ate
or shun or ate
the sun
the tongue
become golden.

He ate
the sun, was *vey*
porized.

*

Lapidary.
Lapidoggy
little dogie   dairy   *la pide*
asks

for it, milk of memory
the life of mammals.

*

Fault
falls down   the downy
hillside
blême   blameless.

What could be softer than this crack in the rock?

*

Flow floe flower flux flumen flume fume font funnel refurbish furbelow
and above, glissando glider patination pasturize pastoso,
en el campo
hay plaquetas tenemos
plástica, pichones vuelan de la hierba cuando anda la gente en botas
          románticas
las faldas pesantes y mojadas de las damas cuelgan insectos y serpientes
          y los nidos abandonados construidos de flores.
No tiene el campo nada después, después
el río repleto de cosas ablandadas por el agua y la gravedad. Qué edad
          tienen las niñas que flotan en el diluvio?

*

Sauce a sort of fate, we say.

He talks and talks in the hope that something will happen
to create an ending.

*

aghast ghastly ghostly August a gust
the ghost of Augustulus, a pygmy
among Romans.

*

Valve *veyihiyeh* a valuent an effluent oh happie
happie
pair perhaps a pear or
pared
a hand in the rubble making sense
of it. What we know become center, what we come to know
disposed around it. A hand
protrudes from a hill of stone as if the body strove to rise
as if drowning
as if the project were to turn stone to liquid.
Or saying : "this hill is mine," or, "hale," or
hieratic gesture, or merely
at the point of death summoning the dog to play.

*

The deadman's hand
proclaims the land.

*

Burnt-umber undercoat
and a scumbled surface
reds and greens

as if incandescing, as if
glow-in-the-dark
psycho
delic dis, or
dys
placed is this
ok is this per
mitted, what kind
of mitt per
what?
Watt? Coll
lated, with milk may be beside
the sea, sidled up to the beau-
tiful sea or
tolled to lead
o! ended
by water.

*

Because accustomed to a set of pronouns
like dress or a cut of hair
a way to walk or run
a piece of body
a set of glands
as if to say
pronouns
is fate. An evil inherent
in becoming accustomed to one or another.

*

I knew a woman who slept with the entire history department,
Professor Joe
on Mondays, etc., "but Sundays
I keep for myself." She would caress my hand
when she passed the salt.

What are the outlets for that kind of talent?

She told me I would have to wait,
but I was next in line.

*

Thirteen ways of looking at a blackboard.
The privilege of washing a stone.
Understanding that within the rubble there's a unity of intention, a
palimpsest.

In the depths was a motive or at least a motif.

Staggering through leafy darkness—hark!
What harkens? The cliff in silhouette
as if seen sideways, was somehow
smaller,
feminine,
moon,
dog,
detritus,
demented,
delimited.
At the edge of the cliff
At the deep cleft

At the impulse to scramble downwards
upwards
downwards
ins Grüne   wet spring
the ooze of what process set in motion when I step there
my hand rested against granite
dripping with watercress, every thing
changed, or
imperceptibly.

*

One wants the species fellowship.

*

Breasting the wave we say put your weight
on one leg, then
the other, your weight
where it matters. We say
there will be a guiding hand,
a respite, but don't
count on it.

*

Having spent a decade fixated on the backs of knees
and another on the folds of flesh when she turns her neck
and another on tendrils of hair and the struggle
between civilization and chaos in the way she wears it.

The thing about the ephemeral is that it's ephemeral. That's
what gets you. The thing about the ephemeral
is that it's ephemeral.

Country Matters: Four Poems

1
Lean season. A fox,
the male,
pries a sheet of roadkill
from the frozen tarmac.

2
On the Utah-Wyoming line a sign: CAUTION—
MIGRATION ROUTE, and as I round the bend
the carcasses of incautious deer and a big white Great Pyrenees,
red muzzle deep in the entrails of an otherwise intact
cadaver,
the sheep on the hill and the wolves
for the moment forgotten.

3
Hair of the dog, like homeopathy
or magic—coopting the enemy's
power.

4
Yesterday evening I dined on venison.
In the morning the garden
was a field of stubble.

IV

Different Birds

Different Birds

San Diego   Away from home, and other teeth will eat my tomatoes.
Faithless, anyone's
tomatoes.

Butterfly almost the color of the oleander blossom
it lands on. Slightly greener, but wings folded
become invisible. Something here,
must be, eats
butterflies.

Scant rain
big drops
with space between
nonetheless
one would think
a hammer-blow
to a hummingbird.

A second generation of flowers on my night-blooming
                    cereus
waits for dark, and in the valley between its ridges
tiny snails search for nutriment.

Cock-eye the Sailor Man
a port in every girl.
Just have to learn the sandbars.

Sydney,   Like home? Two cockatoos perched on a phone line.
Coogee Bay

And a walk, still dazed with travel,
along cliffs and beaches, Coogee to Bondi. Coogee
an arch of sand between promontories.

Cemetery Cliff terraced above surf. A wheel
to steer by, three spokes intact.
"He sees his pilot face to face
Now he has crossed the bar"
Captain George Nyholm 11th December 1907
Aged 55.

Lorikeets.

Magpies, but larger than ours, and perch in trees.
Blue-lit public bathrooms.
Junkies can't see their veins. One would think
they'd miss.
Or skin-pop. Or even
mark a vein before entering.

Katoomba,   Like a white rag
Blue Mountains cockatoo flutters down the canyon.

Silently the white cockatoo
like a leaf
floats
to canyon bottom
the merest lint
in the shape of a bird
on the green mat
of eucalyptus.

60 years to get here,
skating all the way.
And how many left
for the rest.

The unfamiliarity of the southern sky.

"Sailors take warning."

In the morning

In the morning al amanecer at the becoming
day   the light,
understood as progress,
not mandate, declares
it will happen
in the face of all logic.

Fell, like a handkerchief
with wings.

Coogee Bay   Concrete pools filled by the tides.

"Beautiful"–alright, then.

The niceties of daily life.
Society a loose bond of friendships.

The sand drained from beneath her feet she enters
pushing the waves before her, become liquid,
dissolved, resolved
as vector.

The half-life of life.
A discontinuous life experienced as discontinuous.

A gull flies low across the beach
its shadow before it
broken by the surface it seems
to paint.

Sydney   Jewfish.
First time I've seen one on a menu, and I order it
as if compelled, my head

thrust forward, reptilian,
checking the room for danger,
without, and within. The fish
named for the way it rubs its pectorals,
for all the world a moneylender
rubbing his hands,
anticipating the ruin
of another Christian. Shylock
the Jewfish. Rationale
for the deaths of millions.
What would I call it,
swallowed insult? Eucharist
of humiliation? Delicious and tender,
with an avocado chutney.

Here as elsewhere,
the scourge of Christianity.

A short black/ a tall
black. It's only coffee,
only here.

Gippsland,
Phillip Island

Songs of unfamiliar birds

unfamiliar birds and their songs

pharaonic birds
magpies
that warble
in the spring

raven, but with a different call
(called "crow" here)
the cry of a child
wah   wah
wah

many ibis grazing among black cattle
scarlet and turquoise rozellas
kookabarras
kangaroos
wombats
wallabies
tree de
cline and fall
terns
the ocean turqoise   at the far end
indigo
shearwater
muttonbird
gulls with cinnabar beak and feet and black
black unblinking eyes
a giant worm.

A plank stairway down the bluff, weathered
to the gray of the sky. Beneath the slats
nesting penguins, and
dead penguins also.

Melbourne   MELBOURNE GIRLS

1
This is the child of fairytales: blond,
angular, eight years old,
red jacket, turquoise pants, on a green
bench, and strokes
a bunny.
Twitchy nose.

Isn't this embarrassing?
Think of the passions of children
think of a passionate childhood
a moment of stasis belying the violence.

Was that violins, or the screech of a tram wheel.
Clang.

In the Victoria market
one could buy such.
And there may be others,
each identical.

Where is the complex life
of the magic child?

2
Who does she see in her mind's mirror,
the day's confection of darkened lashes
or the pallid animal that washed its face
at bedtime? Right now
licks the foam from a coffee spoon
and talks to her boyfriend who thinks
"foam is foam, is good enough." Quoth she,
"wha' evah,"
and flips her hair.

3
Time's transit so fast and I catch myself wondering
who put the dot on the i
and for what reason. "The real
Australia,"
she says, as if reality
were anywhere we don't inhabit. Enough reality
for anyone.

Anti
podes.

Tipped over, as if
the brain every so often attempted
to right itself.

Nighttime sculling the Yarra River.

Them and the ducks.

Singing as a matter of muscle and breath.

Nolan: "…it was not mummified in the belief
that God is a drover."

This catastrophe befalling an entire continent.

To worry endlessly about being Australian. Imposed
on the landscape. The Sistine Chapel
of despair. So that the light
emerges.

Little black ducks with a white
something above their beaks:
the local grebes.

Sculling clubs upon Yarra.

All-girl crews in blue-and-white jerseys the cox in red
and on a bike path a coach with a bull-horn "square
your shoulders, girls."

All manner of birds not known—this one
the size of a small pigeon white underside black
        back and bib the rest pied, feeds
on the bank, the beck of bug
and worm, the look of a bug-and-worm-eater.
I make it fly so as to see
the white stripe of its wings. Elegant
black legs and eyes. Right next to me it grabs a worm
and swallows. A magpie
lark. Hark
hark.

Knees to chest the breast
flattened, vulva
presented. "And
stroke!"

Make a muddy track
by the river.

Presuppose that it's dusk
and cloudy
on the cusp of spring,
the city all around us.

Black swans with red beaks, at the tip
a horizontal band of white.
They feed on grasses.

The generative triangle.

Only so many ways
to make a wall stand up. Count
them.
Let's pile
a thing on a thing the lives
like ants
stomp stomp
who's to answer for.

I will ascribe a thought to a house (a horse),
a submissive gesture to a kangaroo, its hands
clasped, as if to say,
"please."

"Of course it suits you."
In the company of noses.

In the cathedral:

"Whether you have entered this church to pray, out of
  curiosity, or merely because of the rain, welcome."

Outside, Flinders in bronze in the bow
of a bronze boat, clear-eyed, impeccable
in the bronze garb
of a Georgian gentleman, the boat buoyed
not upon waves but on the straining forms
of anonymous brutes. And truth be told,
unwittingly.

"I think that angels are natural creatures
that you can't see. Like giant squid."

Wilpena   Dusk: big reds
Pound,   gallahs and
Flinders   ravens.
Range

Stock-still the roos could pass
for eucalyptus stumps.

Hard black pellets the size of a half-dollar.

Nao problems.

Frosty dawn the grass frozen.
Kangaroo retreats through the eucalyptus.

Dime-sized yellow balls with thorns.
Nao worries.

Outside my tent a joey
is separated from its mother
by a low fence. Her body
strains forward in silent
anguish. I summon a ranger
to reunite them.

This may be a begging routine.
I may have been conned
by a kangaroo.

How could I learn what I've learned if I'd learned other
        things?

From Blinam camel trains
of copper. Now
a kangaroo and claret pie.

Emulation: emu see, emu do.
Or, to kill a bird, emulate it.

Low moon stripes the forest. All night mynahs
talk and talk, elaborating a theme.

Hopefulness instinctive in the young.
Otherwise there would be no children.

In the room full of eating people a small child
wanders, in pursuit
of whatever curiosity. Her father
follows with his eyes, alert, prepared
to rescue. "Give her some rope,"
he thinks, and I think to tell him
that as long as life lasts alert to danger
his eyes will follow her.

Thin wash of green over burnt red earth.

By the side of the road the remains
of a kangaroo, half-gone, a bit of flesh
darkening the otherwise bleached ribs, the low arch
of vertebrae. Where a truck
left it. Its head intact,
though eyeless, and it seems to scream

the agony of all that live. The stench
of putrefaction covers it
and everything around it.

flinders (fl n d rz) *pl.n* Bits; fragments; splinters.
What the mountains are made of.

A pair of wedgetail eagles on a dead sheep
fly low to the ground at my approach. A magpie,
desperate, flees, thinking
the eagles have plans for it.
Not this time.

Emu paté—perfumy aftertaste
kangaroo fillet, camel sausage
emu pattie, bacon on top,
over mash
ryeberry coulis and deep-fried
parsnip.

Some would do it anyway
for God's command,
despite the pleasure.

Kangaroos abounding

Adelaide   At the Eros Restaurant the pretty waitress stands
with her left (her off)
hand coiled
behind her, covering
the cleft. A peculiar
modesty—in tight black pants
slung low, and she's unbuttoned
her white shirt to reveal
both breast and belly.

The way a swan will float
sometimes, a leg
resting on its back.

A long blond swan.

Something to do with a hand, then.

A couple eats silently. It's clear he experiences her jeans
as an affront, as things aren't great
between them.

The problem with feral olives,
the radio says, is that the natives
haven't a chance
against them. And these on the table
are small, hard,
camphory.

A bad copy of Canova's Cupid and Psyche on the wall,
but the intention pure enough. And a frieze of dancing
girls.

Curtin Springs   Curtin Springs
A few buidings, and a corral for the camels.
1700 square miles
1000 cows.

"As long as we can run a few cattle and tourists…"

90% of the land burnt over.
"Careless aborigines," he says, or maybe
"to clear a space of snakes. Hard to know why
they do anything. Fifty thousand years
and they didn't even
invent the wheel."

Unroll my bag in red dust and watch the stars.

Clouds to the south and west from blue to purple
and there, pure light, she comes
above the horizon.

One sliver to the east
invisible before
incandesces, the bark on the eucalyptus
cuprous
burnished
the gallahs explode in song and the earth
returns to red again, my shadow
an enormous pincer.

It's a three-gallon kettle the slight girl pours from,
pewter, or the color of pewter, no-
nonsense, industrial,
a thick stream of boiling water.

The pepper has four holes
the salt has one, but larger.

Rehearsed words.
Two doctors, orthopedist and
"my anaesthetist,"
motorcycling from Darwin to Adelaide.

The anaesthetist's
the quiet one.

A bird's life
blown by the wind.

During the night some insect
has bitten me—a round swelling
above the joint of my right thumb.

Harder than a mosquito bite, no apparent center, but
there it is. Nothing deadly, despite
the possibilities.

We think the holy of holies of all peoples
should be open to curiosity.

Uluru and Kata Juta.
Kata Juta The two great thighs bisected
by a line of green.

"The men would jerk off here?"
"That too."

Shallow caves   omphalic,
feminine, or
omphalopian.

Where rain has streaked them with
illegible hieroglyphics.

It's about entering.
It's about emerging.

A man and a woman, very old, each hold
a hand of a still older man to steady him as he staggers
up slope into the gap.
They reach the first resting place.

I can imagine being some day both grateful and
            resentful of benches.

Flinty sunlight.

Each with its thin crown of soil and greenery.

The encapsulation of space otherwise limitless to the eye.

A charcoal forest amidst burnt brick the clouds white and
gray drifting through deepest blue and the thin fringe of
soil and greenery
like a cap sits atop each monolith.

A hillside of cobbles, grass
and live and burnt
shrubs. Very pale
occasional
lavender flowers
or pale green shoots.
Multicolored.
Vivid as glass.

Resting, I exchange a few words with a Japanese couple
stopped for a picture, and suddenly there's a set of social
        obligations
of which I'm unaware that render parting
awkward—a gesture I'm supposed to perform
but haven't learned.

Hawk teeters on the wind.

Just past dawn, and
so many galahs feeding on the bush one could think they
        grew there.
Festooned with galahs.
So the landscape becomes a textbook for the behavior of
animals and animals a textbook for the behavior of humans.

An aboriginal woman whose English would indicate
that as a child and into adulthood she spoke none
speaks now on her cell phone in her own language in a
        place
where in her girlhood all tools
were wood or stone.

Imagine a people whose primary identity is social—the individual a very limited concept—my role is who I am. Then the cataclysm and the foundations of the society suddenly crumble or at least are revealed as insufficient for the new reality. Survival becomes a matter of experiencing one's primary identity as individual. Only the most aberrant—those most aberrant in the threatened society—succeed quickly and easily. For the rest generations of despondency, at a loss (and lost) in the new landscape.

The change from self to "self" as if limbs ripped off.

Justice is right ordering, and honor
one's place in that order–one's
rights. One's
rightful place.
Henry Adams:
whatever your class you will be trained for a society
that will no longer exist by the time of your initiation.

Wanampi, the water snake, swims across his pond
            through spangles
of tourist coins.

Mulga and witchety instead of mesquite.

Mistletoe a parasite of each. Snotty-gobbles.

How did these aquatic bugs
get here from the last waterhole?

King's Creek   Dingo scat but no dingoes.

Crested pigeons.
The courting of noisy minahs.
Flaccid camels at midday.

Maybe 60 stations in the NT. This one turned tourist
   hostel.

EU and Commonwealth kids can stay for a year, allowed
to work "to aid travel," but for no more than three
months at any job. The idea, presumably, that a short
gig wouldn't displace a native worker. So the tourist
industry is inhabited by an endless supply of cheap labor
—at Kings Creek Station 10 languages working together.
And of course a certain percentage decide to settle—
attracting the "right" immigrants must be a part of the
concept.

How could anyone who has seen them in the wild
bear to keep one in a cage?

This evening, sitting on a lit porch, the cockatoo caged
in chicken wire not 20 feet away insistently begs my
attention, "hello," in the captor's language. Humans are
its life, provide their careless silence in the absence of
the flock that is home and family. A creature of trees
and crowds here forced into nightlong solitude. It grips
the wires of its cage, as close to me as possible, insufficient
as I am to meet its hunger.

The cruelty of keeping zoo animals in this environment,
captured in sight of their pens for the amusement of
         tourists.
Careless brutality.

To measure one's life by a dog's or a star's.

The wisdom of my people—that at the heart of greatest joy
is greatest sorrow, memory being
the plague it is.

I chat with a couple in a caravan. My age, give or take. The wife offers me her seat by the fire. I demur. She insists—"I'll be doing things anyway." Not ten minutes later an ungodly wailing, the words gradually understood something about no place to sit. They've downed a fair bit of whiskey. I stand up, so does he—the universal embarrassed moment, his loyalty and comfort in conflict with the moment's pleasure. I say, "Sounds like your wife needs you," and retreat to my sleeping bag.

Coffee in hand, walks around. Where's a table? Puzzled.
      Face like a mask.

A sweet young thing with a nervous laugh
he thinks will make
the days pass quickly.

Only the joys of the weefolk untainted.

Hey pigeon!
Nice landing!

Kings Canyon   Mannerly trees.
Discrete plants inhabit their places
each within its patio of sand.

What significance, if any,
to the ragged black cloth
draped on a fallen bough?

Ghost gum, white pine
exploit the cracks.

Desert   grass   tree

No two places no two moments alike
each a cinder
lit and extinguished.

The endless holocaust that will have its end
at the end of everything
in entropic distance.

Cycads   fernlike   palmlike   survivors

Not quite in any sense the goat I was,
nonetheless I save myself when I trip
and slide
onto the scree. Only a little cost
to weathered tendons.

My own shadow trapped
amid the odd linear shadows of desert plants.
A frenzy of wind.

Toward the end of his life my father asked me, "Why
do you always have to do things
your own way?" and I laughed, not aware
there had been a choice.

Poetry first and foremost
a tool for knowing.

No time to note
everything. One makes perhaps
the wrong choices,
but so it is.
I was thinking for instance, when I tripped,
of the Irish kid
behind the breakfast counter. From Kerry,
she said, and I'd forgot to tell her
about my time in Skibbereen,

the car broken, waiting at roadside
for the rental company. Hard to know what's not
significant. A dirty edge of town,
an oily ditch by the road,
horse-drawn wagons hauling metal.
And here I am at the base of a canyon,
pancakes of sandstone,
in the dead center of Australia,
wind whipping
strange trees. If I'm very careful
I can parse their sounds.
Olive-green, yellow grasses—
millet, I think—sprays of flowers,
orange, yellow, occasional blue,
and stumps of charcoal from the last burn
in the overwhelmingly red landscape.

To the West Twenty-six wild camels. I walk among them
MacDonalds and they amble off, small groans from those forced to rise.
Ur of the Chaldees.

Like me, the first of them, transported
from Arabia, might have thought,
"Not so bad, a lot like home."
Sky ahead red with blowing sand.

Through every dry watercourse
a flood of red sand, and the sky to the south and east
something between pink and purple.
450 K to my next campsite,
another night under stars, unless the wind
prevent it. Though certainly a tent would be useless
in such a gale.

All manner of leaf and twig blowing.

Helen Gorge   Due south a great starless blackness,
like Poe's negative where black was white and the savage god
inhabited an ultimate warmth within the frozen antipodes.

I sit here waiting for the dingo I've been told is in the habit
of coursing the sand, unlikely as it seems
that so hunted a beast
would pass before its hunters.

All over Australia poison baits are offered
for its eradication. It's not really native, one hears
repeatedly, probably came with the aborigines, no more than
50,000 years ago, maybe less, as little as 3
millennia. So authenticity becomes a matter
of choosing the moment and killing all
that follow. By that logic, why not poison
the aborigines, why not the europeans, leave the land clean
of all but birds, reptiles, and marsupials?

High-pitched electric squeak of a bat.

Alpha Centauri and its mate still above the cliffs, but the
                cross
lost from sight. South, however,
exactly where it was.

In this desert drought's
the only news, flocks trimmed
by two-thirds, and a good lamb
goes for 150 that last year would have fetched
a third of that.

The line articulated
so as to express volume.

High up a plane deadheads for Canberra. Down here
the rumble of engines. What can the creatures
make of it?

The wind's died down
to a downy breeze, enough to keep
the flies away.

Cliff. Absence of stars
is how you know it's there.

La Chingada and La Llorona stalk
the dreams of Mexicans,
cause and effect
to the very edge
of the fiesta.

Glen Helen at dawn
a pair of black birds—
cormorants—loonlike
on the water.
Silver fish—bream—
leap for their breakfast.

Clucking and trilling on the cliffs, the galahs
arrive. They sing
for the insistent moments of mating.

13 grebe and one chick.
Through the cloud the light silver
then gold in the clearing.

Ormiston   Up a long incline and around a hill, into a canyon, then
Gorge   opens
onto the Pound, wide floodplain, a lake once—one can see
along the mountains the mark of old beaches—reduced,
                as now, to a series of deep, cold,
shadowy pools in an expanse of rock and sand. The
                Finke River,
salvation of seabirds, and once
a songline.

There are fish, a sort of bream, that grow a foot long and die
when the pool dries but always reappear
with rain.

Ants everywhere, red sand
for soil, a ready-made pigment.

A cut through the mountains at a bend of the dry bed.
            At the outer edge a cliff
undercut by a still crescent of water, and on what would
be the slow side, the eddies, pink sandstone broken into
            square terraces. Emerging, the largest pool,
in places cut beneath the hill, but on the other side a
            wide beach, and on it
some kids from America and some aborigines, teenagers
from a mission school, volunteers and their charges,
down from Darwin to show their land to the natives
and bring them a god. Such
perfect innocence, innocent of the temptation
of irony and of all temptations.

I want to tell them, "whatever you do
you'll never do again." Despite joy
or sorrow.

Alice Springs   Water from "the bore," the deep well that's the only
            source, here,
and in the continent's entire center. Brackish,
pleasant, like certain mineral waters.

A country where one needn't add salt at table.

"Beautiful," the waitress says
as she writes down my order.
Red Ochre Grill—Alice—
Morton Bay Bugs with a spicy kim chee,
the vinegar cut with parsley.

Camel sirloin with butternut squash, called pumpkin
　　　here.

As sacrament,
flesh of my flesh that carried Abraham
forth from beside the river.

Alice Airport　　Foreign presence in Alice overwhelmingly German,
then Italian and French. Plane to Darwin late, but Alice
Airport's actually pleasant—reasonable prices, outdoor
tables, a small lawn to sprawl on, magpie larks, plaintive
ravens, and a small garden of native plants. One walks
onto the runway to board, apparently.

No daypacks then, no backpacks,
slacks on women some places illegal, shorts
more so. Midriffs never bare. So the girl facing, reclining
　　　against her chair,
legs spread, hands clasped behind her head, naked from
　　　hip to breast, and a small
glittery stone in her navel says "look at me," in jeans,
　　　t-shirt and
flipflops—nothing unusual, but the change so fast
that those my age are constantly overcome by wants
　　　to which we've developed
no defenses.
　　　　　What a drag
　　　　　　　　　it is.
Hell, she couldn't even have sat that way, nor her mother,
beside her, neither.

I had forgotten about her for a while, but find myself
now on the grass behind her. She stretches forward—
　　　a purple thong.

Removal of a pullover
attended by much drama.

From the air
vegetation in the lee of red dunes
marks the pattern of ancient seabeds.

A road through a desert almost devoid of vegetation
pinker than the burnt land around it. One billabong
visible. Must be the bed of an ancient lake. On its edge,
just into a greener place, a square of farmland, different
colors, green to rust, and all right-angled, like a set of
tiles. Down the road the messiness of a small settlement,
twenty buildings and an air strip.

Mountains like mudpies
brown amidst the red.

A haze of pink above the desert from a three-day wind.
Feels almost like there's no way to take in enough liquid.

Now the desert a set of parallel streaks
one dense red-ochre dry waterhole
and higher ground a gray-green stain on the land but at
        last
a few billabongs.

No blend—boundaries between soil types as if etched.
Even where bisected by a line of ridge the striping, SE to
        NW,
continues, troughs and crests
a shade of color different.
Nothing interrupts the pattern.
Even in higher ground where the broken land
forms a harsh circle you can make it out
as understrate.

More billabongs,
the dry places stained by different concentrations
of blue minerals. And no sign
no sign at all
of human presence.

Patches of low cloud.

From this height the round form could be hill or crater.
Darker center, probably foliage, probably hill or crater.
Salt pans   dry billabongs   a few threads of water.

Heart-shaped, purple.

A spray of vegetation, like the spines
of a fan or the fin of a sailfish.

Interminable striping.

Small clouds, wisps
to cast a shadow. But the haze
that had stood at the horizon
pink as ever
begins to close in.

The stripes are almost gone,
and a straight pink road perpendicular to our path.
Stripes again, but regular. Almost like gouges.

No stripes at all. Wait—
some sort of patterning between dry floodways.

And another road, four bends within my sightline.

The soil more beige than red, more vegetation, though
        hardly lush. One could perhaps run cattle here.

Hey, two roads, three,
scratched into the desert.
And a fourth, a fifth. All drawn
by ruler. The darker heights may be forest. Forested
by no tree I'd recognize.

Now two buildings and an airstrip. Roads. A watercourse,
       in places a trace of water.
The land pocked with circles,
some surrounding blue dots of water.

Major watercourses from arid hills feed into one. The
       soil as revealed by roads red once more in places.

The watercourse a flow of sand, threads of green
       meandering through it.

A plateau breaks into mesas, fingers and islands. The road
twists among them.
A clump of buildings, and a few fields
along a watercourse.
Continuous water, with a road beside it.
And another still, the band of riverine greenery wider.

Fields, and the glint of a laminate roof.
Ploughed striations. The soil
a set of earthtones,
different yellows and reds. More billabongs. Two
       buildings. More fields,
five buildings surrounded by trees. In the distance,
       across a mesa,
a field of half-circles. A series of fires.
And a river
enters the sea.

The ugly slurry of mines.
A small town with trees and parallel streets.

A riverbed thick with trees and a dozen farmsteads.
Network of roads. A larger town. A full billabong. A
        hilltop home. Another mine pit. A paved
highway with a truck train and three cars, two of them
        passing.
A large reservoir and a lake fringed
with algae.

Big rivers enter an enormous bay, in its great arms
a ship.
Coming in low over sparse forest, but river beds,
mangrove and swamp.
A bridge across a river and the trail
of a pleasure craft.
Over city now but lots of bush, the airport ahead.
Plots of industrial forest,
other plots scraped bare. Paved roads. A grassy field
with rugby players.
Palm trees. A mall.
Brush. Dry season grasses. The marks of dirt bikes.
And touchdown.

Darwin   At Mindl Beach electric digeridoo gets all the attention.
Four aboriginal girls sing "I'm a believer" while an old man
keeps time with a rock and sings
in his own language and three others
almost skeletal
on the ground in a circle, singing, and another four
sing their music, but it's the white guy
with the drums behind him and the amp and the three
        digeridoos
who takes in the shekels, the others
unquiet ghosts in their own country.

Tapara asked for the body of his lover's son, but Puru-
kupari told him, "no, now that my son is dead we will all

follow him. Everyone will die." And they fought. Tapara became the moon. Then Purukupali took his son in his arms and walked into the sea, where the whirlpool swallowed them. Impassive, the pelicans looked on.

The myths are mute because everyone knew their meaning. So that the girl abducted by pirates—why belabor it? A life of servitude and longing. Her family on the shore, no need to say it, except,
"we looked for her everywhere, but she was gone. They must have stolen her."

"And that among these truths are death, slavery
and thoughtless destruction."

No one who had seen them in the wild could keep them
        as pets,
one would have thought, as if there were limits
to the selfishness of desire.

A culture defined by a pose or a stance,
kouros to contraposto.

Here where once a hill
a pile of stones.

Clastic fields,
hoodoos.

In the paintings animals are indicated by their tracks,
        and people
by the horseshoe trace where they had sat, crosslegged,
as they still do on the streets of Darwin.

Kakadu   A pictograph—the dingo-headed woman—distended
        labia—at the edge of the precipice.

Some things one delights in,
pandanus,
sand palms,
a troglodyte cave with remains of humans. On the mesa
a pool with water lilies.
What the dog told him. Marrawati,
the eagle,
the transport of souls.

And here on the rock at the edge of the flood plain, the girl
had eaten flesh of barramundi at her time of month,
and the people of that place had beaten her, and her
own people came with spears and a world
ended in conflict. A rock
that could be Ilion, how an argument over a woman
ruined everything. In the river
endless bodies for the sisters who had learned,
for their unbridled hunger, to transform themselves
to crocodiles.

A tropical depression.
A notebook full of birds and marsupials.
Goanna.

The choice is always with us isn't it.

Darwin   The girl from Guantánamo to whom all Cubans sing,
what do we have,
not even a picture, she lives
as an essential longing, she
so far from the capital,
as if another life. We live,
she says, as if in scenes
played parallel
on the same stage, she says,

and sways away
from beach to forest.

What a strange thing to write in Darwin
in this other tropics.

Circle round it.
Circle round it.
Flagons of water
as a matter of course.

There were two of us here.
ok   ok
ok
ok.

Sometimes the ship has truly sailed.

V

Dark Season

Canta y no llores

1

Every morning for 10 years 10,000 Greeks took a shit and went out to fight.
Three million six hundred fifty thousand dumps, and Scamander
ran brown in the morning, red
in the afternoon. Plus horses
sheep and cattle.

That, and the carnage.
They leveled forests
to burn the bodies.

Greeks bearing gifts?
A no-brainer.

Dropping a cat into a nest of birds.

Sow the ground with salt,
leave nothing for longing,
no stone on stone.

2

A sense of competence of sorts
in the doggy pleasure of obedience.

Thwack, and the arc of the ball.

The rise and fall of breath.
The celebration of meat and fat.

Grip the ground as if climbing.
As in the reciprocity between pose and painting,
the channeling of impulse and instinct.

3

If I make the effort the crying child
will become white noise.

We only learn betrayal from the best of friends.

Symmetry
and the disappointment of symmetry.

De facto segregation of the back-country.

Let webs be webs
and ivy ivy.
A sense of "not here."

4

Think of satisfaction as a glyph.

As for instance, the woman with distended labia
stopped here,
at the edge of the cliff, where now there's a falls,
and pissed.

Her nose, they say,
was "ladylike."

And her feet glistened with rain.

Corresponding to the tendency of the toes of each foot to resemble each
        other.

A different vocabulary.
These, if I so choose, are my people.

In the darkest of times
creatures of sunset and sunrise.

Edifice erected upon instinct.
Distinction between song and sound.
Busyness of birds.

We kill to assert our right to do so.

Came closer, parted the hairs, squinted.
A set of instructions.

A flurry of gestures,
expression of race place species and self,
invented rituals, every possible
of the moment's dances.

The game of pots and kettles.

As the child builds the components of understanding.

Where was I? Each chamber
like the last.

5
At the end of time
the cattle, freed, revert to aurochs,
docility culled
by coyotes and wolves.
The eye stilled of its restlessness.

Stillness invented.
Come, I will give you meat and fat.

A history of shoes.

Chaotic interplay of fixed positions,
nuance
teased out like a fright wig.

Why appear in a state of constant surprise?
Sand,
and a quiet surface, the bay
nonetheless a battlefield.

Let us imagine the harmonious workings of violence
as if observed from Chaucer's cloud. Small beings
reduced to consequence.
As if to leave no footprint.

Different Stories

1
The man who lives in boring times
bucket by bucket moves a mountain.

Wedded to the trajectory,
a collection of shattered lenses,
a matrix of rituals.

Man, or machete.
A catalogue of expectations.
Cutlass, for instance,
the brute violence of the toolshed
become a scimitar in the hands of pirates.

2
On the subway platform the girl sways
to invisible music.
Maybe she's gone to the islands.

Different stories.
I knew a girl whose childhood
was her mother's experiment
in elective surgeries to make her
"beautiful," new nose, new eyelids,
as the world sees it.
Except that she'd refused the last experiment.
A different story. And what became
of all that perfection,
that one defiance,
that vote for symmetry.

3
Failure to make circles.

Old age, as the young man assured me,
is a state of mind.

In the order of things
there will be fire.

Ownership of islands will be swept by the sound
and all these wetlands.

This has been home
and this has been home
and this has been home.
Much of what you plan for
won't happen, and what does
you'll be unprepared for.

Following beasts,
elk and elephant providing wisdom.
"Where grass is good
there will be meat."
"Salt is aggressive
and rises to water."

4
Mist
and mystery
in the English
idiom, math
and mastery
in the physics of war.

5

A nice day,
flaxen girl in flat sandals licks
a cone of white ice cream
and strides through the park.

Strides through the park in flat sandals
licking a cone of white ice cream.
So nice a day. She eats
white ice cream.

Oh custard.
Oh sugarplum.

6

A Mayan woman with her Mayan children
at the Delacort fountain.
Hard to imagine a beauty more divorced
from that belle époque fragility, she
recalling blood and viscera.
But her children
will speak the local dialect.

7

A tendency to swallow whole when excited
(a tendency to excitement)
but masticate, grind,
that the chestnut not
become the death of you. Chew
as if your life
depended on it.
Time enough for the visible world
beyond the restaurant.

8

In his will he endowed a fund
to feed a homeless person once a year
the finest, most expensive,
and record
the recipient's despair
thereafter.

9

Gleaning the last of an insufficient harvest, he
chops down the final bit of scrub so that his child
will have warm food. Who knows
what luck might bring
to keep them for another day.

First worry,
then despair.

Maybe the last
of insect or mammal
will descend upon them.

Where blond means enough to eat
and brunette not so much.

10

So it turns out
that we're not the answer
to the dreams of centuries.

Lope of the hunter from field to forest.

"We have adapted wheat to grow on clouds
and grain to fall like rain."
Laughed, then died, and the living
guess at the joke.

By Way of the Season

1
After its struggle the gazelle
surrenders to the lion's grip, useless
to fight. Does it think then, does it think
"if only I'd dodged to the right. If only.
Maybe next time."
As the cat disembowels it and begins to feed.

Farewell to the hills
Farewell to the herd
Farewell to water hole and tender grasses
And the joy of the young at the teat.

2
At moments when the consequences of choice are upon us we say
"this can't be all there is," but it can. Regret, nostalgia and longing,
on the other hand, are ready gifts, one can live
as if there were choices with no consequences, as if
the life could be unlived
and lived again.

3
Day before Christmas in the supermarket the Stones are singing "Can't
get no satisfaction," but we try & we try & we try & and we try
and we buy something.

4
No way   no way
elusive as wind.

5

Stories and the stories of stories.
A vocabulary of places gathered and left.
Putting death aside, one wonders whether to climb that distant hill, as in
the conservation of matter.
There are so many windows to look through.
Opposite, a building seems to wear as a crown the trees beyond it. Close
one eye or the other
to recover its true flatness. If I say
"rock dove" do you see "pigeon?"

6

No gull rests now on the cross above the church's triangular facade, but
it's apparently a perch reserved for gulls to take turns at.
So much for religion. One prays
to invest oneself in the known and unknown places,
the simplicity of the abandoned and the immanence of ruins.
Ghost-whispers.

"I am the demon that whimpers at night,"
he said, and the pigeons
(or doves) ride even the steepest wires. The oblique
is granted them. Across the street
in front of the travel agency
a gruff Santa makes Christmas noises
in Caribbean Spanish. For a moment I thought it the ghost
rising through the radiator from the apartment below.
He dances now to *The Entertainer* played on a portable keyboard.
Ragtime Spanish Santa from the Dominican Republic.
And what would Dominic have made of this? "Church
of the Immaculate Deception," he might have said. As in
"I bring you pestilence"
he might have said,
an epidemic of grace.

7

That year three virgins bore sons.

Zeus the King displayed his thunderbolts.
Chango fell as a shower of gold.
And Chac arrived as rain.

Where you find it bring joy.

April

1
March Hare?
April there.

2
April's golden braids
were crowned with violets. She was
the Queen of Maybe,
the cruelest kid.

3
May be after April, maybe. Maybe April.

4
January's nobody's name, nor any —ary. Daughters are April,
May, or June.
Boys are named August. Nobody's
named any —ember.

5
April spills, May allows, June is looney.

6
Once the god and the year were born in April.

7
Everyone loveth
Aprille. Ac on a Mai
mornyng,
was it,
the field was filled.

8
Turn it upside down. On the other side
October. April's

retrograde. In April
one gathers wood and shakes
the summer from blankets. In April
a god could begin to die.

9
Flower, then seed. It's April.
Watch your lap, girl.

10
OED. Prill: a runnel, a rill. A whirligig or top. Short for Priscilla. The
rich copper ore which remains after cobbing and separating the inferior
pieces. Verb: to flow, spirt, purl.

11
Enough, then. A month
as swift as
longing. In January
(here), July
(there), time slows, and one could think to live
suspended.

April (October)
ends hibernation.
Bearish, desperate for berries.

History

The imposition of metal shoes
is the least of the horse's hardships.

The sweet disposition of geldings. As a leather bag
testifies to the mortality of cows.

Once by the shape of a hand
you could say which tribe,
which not.

Let us proceed to the emptying of all things.

Scrape of blade on toast,
each teacup carefully chosen.

Take personally the affronts of the past.

Above, dark water.
Below, dark water.
Rises.
Falls.

Once by the shape of the hand
you could tell the land.

Nationhood

1
We wear the same clothes differently.

Death as a boundary disturbance.

The sway of her hips against the gothic.

Man with man
beast with beast
house of blood.

Explaining perspective to the blind.

The occasion of necessity between ping and pong
as tentative as blossoms.

Not to have been shot at or starved
would seem amazing luck
in the world as it's been.

It's this complex engineering called beauty in motion.
A kinship with cows.
The disguise of the native.

The intelligence of a dog
applied indifferently to landscape.

As useful as feet.

Your body's quick intelligence.
All praise for instinctual virtue.

The language of sorrow has an Irish accent
a Jewish accent
a Scottish accent et cetera.

2

Yellow haze of mustard
among cactus and thorn. Salad
for the border-crossers.

Hand to mouth
as easy as

"…and given the times,"
he said…

Noise and predation.

Become accustomed to muscle and bone
where before
skin
and a skein of nerves.

Sticks his finger in his ear
shakes vigorously
clears his throat.

The unknown codes of the law of twos and sevens.

In considering the greatness of this or that ruler
include the accomplishment of questionable goals.

Dark Season

I
I was a prince or princess in another clime.

Either way
the strum of distance,

the path
a marquetry of leaves,

a stuttering of possibilities.
If you're Beethoven, say
di di di dah!
over and over.

If the shoe is rigid
the foot will follow.

Dark night of the foot.
Foot-loose
for evasion.

At the heart of it
the recurrent fantasy
of the end of all things.

Whatever it is that brings one
to the particular flower.

There are the beasts of the field
and the beasts of the forest
and those that inhabit the margin.

Where self-regard is the only claim,

as why in a list
I put which first which last, which last
which first.

II
Small insults to the body
scratches and such
now scarcely noticed that once brought forth
the keenest sorrow.

Transmuting physiology to a love-testament.

Holding a stretch of time and space.

From the scrotal dice cup
and the vulval dice cup.

Sold out to the nearest empire.

Allegiance to a pronoun
and a bureaucratic arrangement.

III
Some are funnier than others
in the world of couldashoulda.

Why do you do me like you do do do.

Wisconsin become an Italian province.
Why not? It's the snowy part,
with bugs. Home, if home were upstream
from anywhere.

No telling.

Her lap stretched forth to receive the harvest.

IV
Here is a pearl of great price
clasped in your palm.

emergent urge urgent tangent demiurge
angular

Her simplicity allows us to reduce her enormous complexity to caring
          and cared for.

An atavistic compassion for one's kind and whatever kind.

The child's inwardness
silent manipulation and repetition of a set of relationships.
What's better
than buttered bread, the clean sheen on a finger? Someday
my feet will reach the floor.

A child's is but to charm.

V
Is it she or her reflection
at the glass door
waiting to enter?

Persistence of a vague disconnect.
A sense of reality as a set of flat planes.

Blond,
for transparency.

In the perfect world
everyone will wear her hair
"just-so."

Nothing, it turns out,
is as simple as one had hoped. How,

given the species,
could it be otherwise?
For instance,
the mating of cows or cats, the business done
and forgotten.

A dog of black and white,
a witness.
Its feet attack the floor
like castanets.

That the noise and the silence contain each other.

Reference, such that the shape of a thumb
says "Flemish," as remembered from this or that painting.

VI
Civilization a decision to piss on one side of the door only.
Or maybe the existence of dogs.

"She was her own country,"
or viscera like the rest of us.

A woman may have three shirts
of her own weaving.
Time to sacrifice the idea of exotic.

VII
The farmer's daughter
knows about milk and honey
and the smell of birth and death.
Cracked porcelain flecked
with clouds
blue as a bell and as noisy.

Be wary of the aunt
in insistent and ant and
sisterhood.
Implode plowed up
a flower flow or
flux

Varieties of clapping, position of thumbs.

Sourwood Mountain's where you find it.
No chickens, lots
of girls.

Misery and glee cohabiting.

Somebody chooses.

Come, now, to the season of lost.

Like trimming sail.
It's about balance and an edge.

VIII
This god grants nothing.
This god grants nothing.

Walking into a stiff wind
he mutters his multiplications
as a sort of charm.

Atop the hill a flag
whips smartly.
Which seems to give direction. For the moment
at this edge of winter
it's merely blazon of the god of winds
who breathes upon it.

Put otherwise,
what's shown is an unsure index.

What do you say to cosmetic innocence?

The richness of redundancy.

From a set of gestures
one constructs a life

IX
Time measured by the king's reign
as space by pace and hand.
A lifetime stacked on a lifetime on a lifetime,
before which
it was a memory of this or that, "that year
when the rain, when the sun,
when the great beast,
when the meat, when the giant fell," when Jack
or Jillness.
Wasn't that a year.

Habitual pattern
of integration. John Frum
summoned from the astral plane by an aircraft, as if
the god could be tricked
by the appearance of things.

Here's an experiment,
a life remembered as lines between signal moments
of change or stimulus, as in
connect-the-dots. Unspoken passages.
An emblem emerging as if by surprise.
Another: the dots are givens,
one bushwhacks the shortest distances. As seen
from whatever plane John Frum reclines on.

X
Blame not the beasts.
The choristers hid snacks beneath their seats.
The bears
ruined the choir.

Over-grazed
laid waste in record time
a limit to the carrying capacity of any land.

By my kind laid waste.

In the list of conquest
nobody numbers the hired hands.

Hard to imagine that the great many
could have survived with all those pigeons, parrots, buffalo.

XI
Alisoun gives way to Marianne
and the world turns.

Nationhood defined as a woman's lovers.

He was handsome, so she ran off with him,
and we slaughtered the men and enslaved the women,
sowed the ground with salt, and boasted
for a thousand years.

Until the burning of sheaves,
hallucination of nearest and dearest.

The story includes the near-extermination of the race
rescued by heroes or determination or the sheer
exhaustion of the others, or
a surfeit of killing, if such were possible.

Sad stories of the deaths of kings.

The grass was free if you didn't count the owners.

It was the end of possibility,
the last bed one would lie in,
so strange is the story.

Because of the penchant of choristers for snacks
the bears ruined the choirs.

When I was a running boy I'd reach an ocean
and run the other way
like a beast in a cage.

Come up against the largest of disabilities.

Change protagonists and see what happens
to all that you value.

A horror at being forgotten
enough maybe to justify
any horror, as who
has forgotten the ravishing of borders?

XII
Pen and paper first and last.
Immigration, want and war.

"Among these people there's no language, though they twitter at each other
like birds, and perhaps to the same effect–displays of mating, territory, rank.

They're spouting babble
for our benefit,
pretending to communicate.
But it's clearly

pretense, like
their masquerade of
society, a dumb-show
with voices. Their gestures,
the movements
of face and hands, their
'speech,' convey
thought, some
say, but few
believe it."

XIII
The difficult is the only stimulus.

She meets
an inquisitive eye.

The pleasure of caring for the simplest needs
of the easily comforted.

Comfort the cloth monkey.

Dignity
and
Dognity.

And what will be left by morning?
Undoing the knot,
the seed
from which.

A troubled dialogue with the concepts
home   family   death.

"A cup of kindness."

Walked into the clouds.

Counting each hair so as to divide them precisely
right to left.

The monkey fled from us because he saw us
as of his tribe.

XIV
Watch the golden child
undone by drudgery,
the coarsening of foot and hand,
wind-chapped, work-chapped,
and imagine a skill or miracle
to lift its estate.
Let them eat stories, he says,
with a flip of the hand.

Let us ignite the god's light,
fat of the beast
in the form of a candle.
Flame for flesh, though to the beast
it matters not at all.

XV
The romantic stories owe their power to disappointed hopes and a few
moments of the delusions of crowds.

Standing on tiptoes is the only choice.

The same cry,
whether victim or victor.

After a decent interval
they carved crude holes for windows in the fortress wall.
They had predicted peace.

The full transcript of an inner voice
dated and indexed.

A two-part weapon
that first releases a fragrant gas productive of sleep.
The second incinerates the sleeper.

XVI
One man's boredom is another's boredom.

The known world ends
and starts again.

Kennst du das Land
where blossoms
drip butter
and the hollows
of trees
are filled with honey.

And groves are for lovers,
and a furrow's a furrow.

Reproachful gaze
of the beaten child.
In sleep retreats to
the reptile mind
where once a bed of leaves.

To the regendering of language.
Cow or bull
bitch or dog
mare or stallion
hen or cock
fox or vixen.

Faced after all these generations of expansion
with the immanence of contraction.

XVII
From this passion
let nothing come.
Let speech be
as mime to the blind.
Mime to the blind silence
to the deaf.

Peculiar glyphs on a neutral background.

In default of other pleasures
let us make of the emptied earth
a garden.

Leave me alone in darkness for a while—
more than enough to be seen when the dream is over.
Obsessed as I've been these past few days
by the thought of a mime troupe, booked by accident
to perform for the blind whose movements
form a complex accidental dance,
some with arms outstretched in mute searching,
some tapping canes, some led
through invisible boxes by mystified dogs.

Break silence
like bread, out of the disorder of mind
a garden
for thought,
forethought
or not.

Here a tree here a tree
here a rock, and here the dogs.

Or put it otherwise, it was noted in many places
that the silent wind sang whatever the fields told it. So: music,
then speech. As a child
finds patterns in a screen, a new sound to rouse the morning.
Proceed to the annulment of the common instinct.

Like an old spaniel
shaped by habitual laughter.
Like tides overlapping.

Loosed,
drawn to gravity.

Be easy
with language.
Glyphs of migration
an arrow an alphabet
a wedge of birds.

XVIII
The black man who dawn to dusk
sits on the nearest bench stops me today
and says: "that damned pigeon
shat on my shoulder."
"Birds have no respect,"
I tell him, and he answers:
"I don't mind if a blackbird does it, it's the pigeons
bother me."

Discrimination transposed to birds. On the hill
behind him there's a trail
of feathers, what's left
of a chickadee,
and a single spot of red,
as if an offering. And farther up, in the forest,
the fresh corpse of a rooster, bound with ribbons, as bribe
for whatever god.

Out of sight of land and beyond soundings.

Sometimes the sensation of liquid   lick it
swarming
swimming.
As if conducting an experiment,
history written in feet and hands
and the growl of language.

Has teeth   has teeth
in it.

What's lost and saved.

Plash of stones across water.

Lightning Source UK Ltd.
Milton Keynes UK
UKHW010627270320
360970UK00001B/13